Cello Time Runners

Piano accompaniment book

Kathy and David Blackwell

Contents

MUSIC DEPARTMENT

OXFORD
UNIVERSITY PRESS

T0057046

1. Start the show
(for Clare)

KB & DB

Rock tempo

The cello book contains several cello duets; these are unaccompanied and so not included here.

3. Heat haze

KB & DB

4. Medieval tale

KB & DB

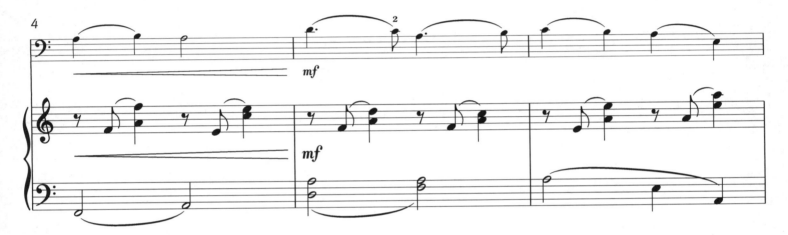

5. Chase in the dark

KB & DB

With menace

6. Spy movie

KB & DB

7. Gypsy dance

KB & DB

9. On the go!

KB & DB

* The repeat is written out in full in the cello part.

10. That's how it goes!

KB & DB

With energy

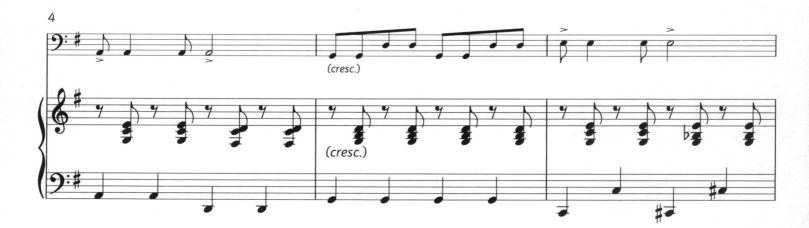

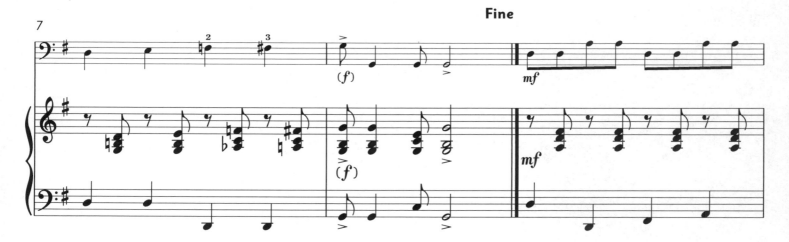

D.C. al Fine

11. Blue whale

KB & DB

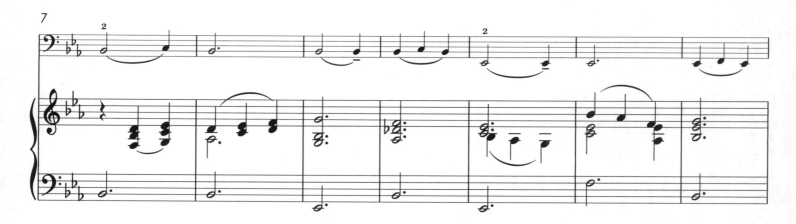

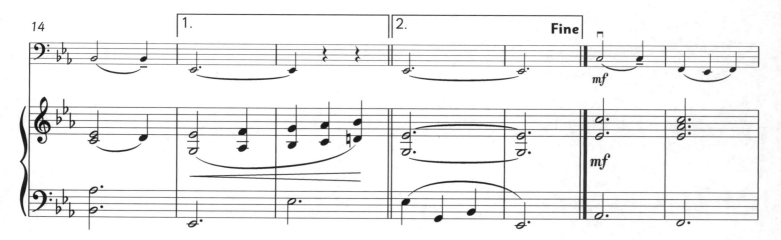

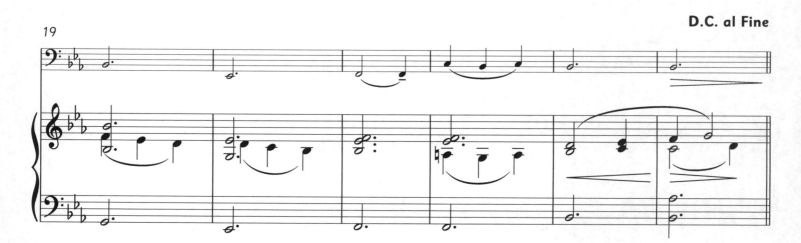

12. Mean street chase

KB & DB

14

13. Allegretto

Mozart

14. Cornish May song

Traditional

16. Prelude from 'Te Deum'

Charpentier

17. Paris café

KB & DB

18. Starry night

KB & DB

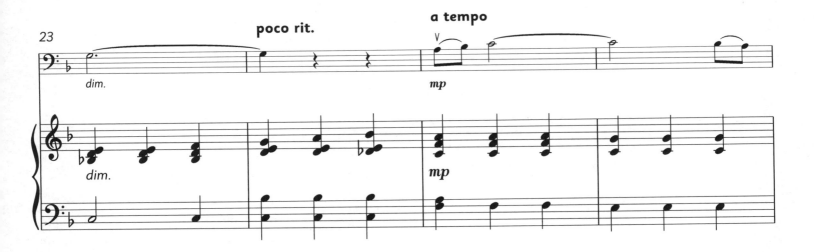

19. Cello Time rag

KB & DB

Not too fast

20. Caribbean sunshine

KB & DB

21. Jacob's dance

KB & DB

22. Song from the show

KB & DB

23. The road to Donegal

KB & DB

Can also be bowed: ♩ ♪ ♩ ♪ | etc.

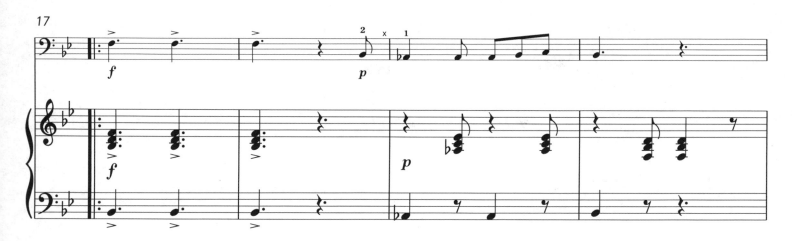

24. Cat's eyes

KB & DB

With menace (Swing)

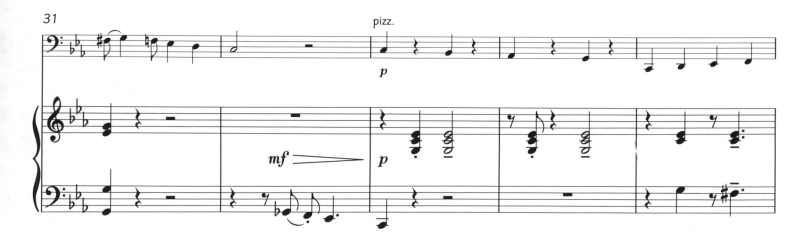

25. Mexican fiesta

KB & DB

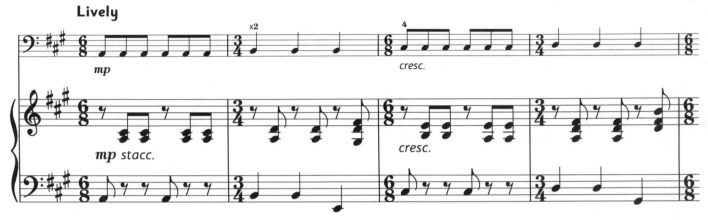

26. Summer evening

KB & DB

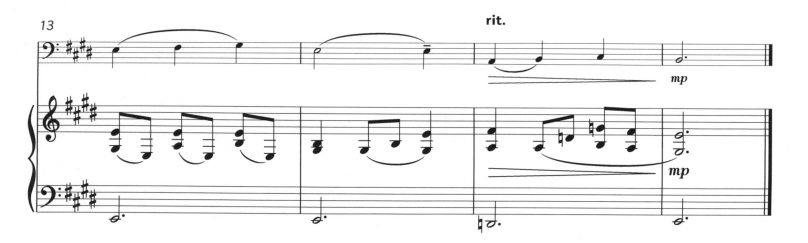

27. Extension rock

KB & DB

28. Show off!

KB & DB

30. One day

KB & DB

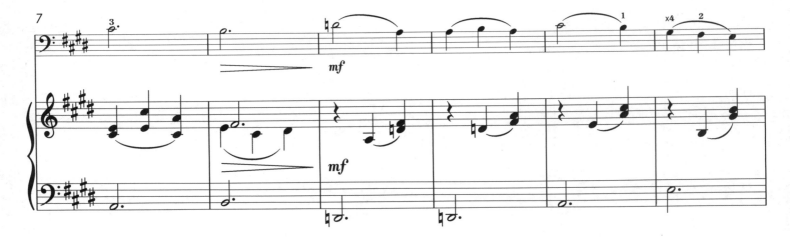

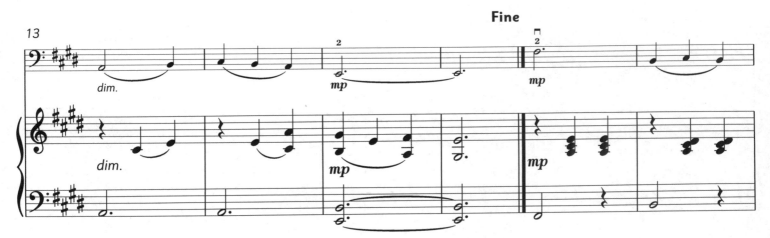

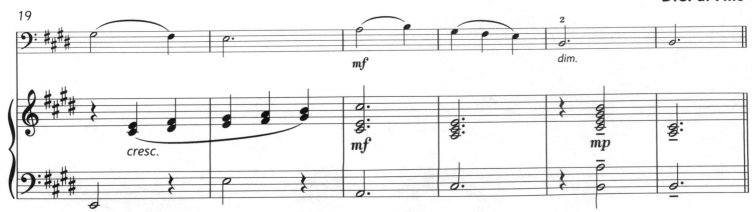

31. Aerobics

KB & DB

32. Hungarian folk dance

KB & DB

33. Show stopper

KB & DB

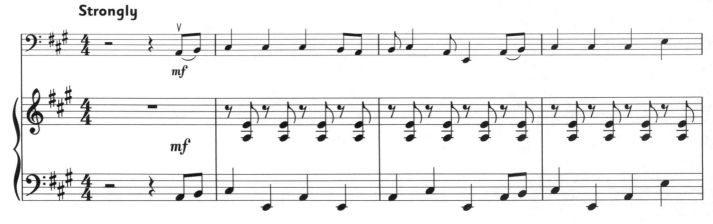

34. Farewell to Skye
(for Iain)

KB & DB